DISCOVERING BIBLICAL TREASURES

UNDERSTANDING MALACHI

A Commentary on the Book of Malachi using Ancient Bible Study Methods - UPDATED

Michael Harvey Koplitz

Published by Michael Harvey Koplitz

Acknowledgments

This work could not have been accomplished without Dr. Anne Davis, who taught me Ancient Bible (Hebraic) study methods, and my two study partners, Rev. Dr. Robert Cook and Pastor Sandra Koplitz. We know the journey has just started and will last a lifetime. The discovery of the depths of God's Word is waiting for us to find.

Table of Contents

Introduction

While I was attending Seminary earning my M. Div. degree, I started to question what the instructors and reference books, which were required, were saying about the Scriptures. One of the ideas being offered then was that the Bible was full of errors and not factual. I found that attitude disturbing for Seminary instructors to be teaching. After all, the Seminary experience is to train pastors to go out into God's world and preach the Bible. How can you preach the Bible if you believe what these instructors are teaching? The methods that were being taught to examine the Bible just seemed inaccurate to me.

After graduating from Seminary, I spent a lot of time reading different views about the Bible. I eventually reached the Zohar. This collection of midrashim are considered the secret work of the Torah, according to Kabbalists. In addition, I read quite a bit about Messianic Judaism. Their view of the Bible differs greatly from the Seminary view.

I decided that the biblical interpretation that was being taught in Seminary was not the biblical interpretation the people heard when Jesus Christ (whose Hebraic name is Yeshua) preached. I went on a quest to learn what the people of Yeshua's day heard, and what they thought when the Scriptures were read. This quest led me to Dr. Anne Davis and The Bible Learning University. Dr. Davis was in search of the same thing I was searching for. She had made numerous discoveries that helped me in my quest. I earned the Ph.D. degree from The Bible Learning University in Hebraic Studies in

Christianity concentrating on ancient Bible Studies methods.

Finally, I found someone who believed that the church has placed almost 1900 years of their theological ideas about the Scriptures, which differed from the original Hebraic thoughts, and in many places possibly misinterpreted its original meaning. What is also important to hear is that the basic tenants of Yeshua as God's Messiah, my LORD and Savior are in the Bible. My faith in Yeshua is stronger now that I have learned from Dr. Davis how to study the Scriptures in the same manner that the people did in Yeshua's day.

I have included some articles that describe the differences between Greek learning methods and Hebraic learning methods. Please do not skip by them as irrelevant, unless you are familiar with the Ancient Bible student method, because if you do, then the analysis and commentary that follows may become difficult to understand.

Our God is vast and so is His Word. May God bless you in your discovery of what God's Word is about.

Malachi was a contemporary of Haggai and Zechariah. They lived during the Second Temple era. Since the book of Ezra does not mention Malachi when addressing Haggai and Zechariah, Radak asserts Malachi is the last of the prophets. Malachi's full identity is not known. There are some quote and opinions about Malachi that can be found in the Talmud.

The Main Difference between the Greek Method and Hebraic Method of Teaching

Once you are aware of the two teaching styles, you will determine if you are in a class or reading a book, whether the analysis and/or teaching method is in a Greek or Hebraic method. In the Greek method, the instructor is right because of advanced knowledge. In the college situation, it is because the professor has his/her Ph.D. in some area of study, so one assumes that he or she knows everything about the topic. For example, Rodney Dangerfield played the role of a middle-aged man going to college. His English midterm was to write about Kurt Vonnegut Jr. Since he did not understand any of Vonnegut's books, he hired Vonnegut himself to the write the midterm. When it was returned to him, the English

Professor told Dangerfield that whoever wrote the paper knew nothing about Vonnegut. This is an example of the Greek method of teaching. Did the Ph.D. English professor think she knew more about Vonnegut's writings than Vonnegut did?[1]

In the Greek teaching method, the professor or the instructor claims to be the authority. If you are attending a Bible study class and the class leader says "I will teach you the only way to understand this biblical book," consider the implications. This method is common since most seminaries and Bible colleges teach a Greek method of learning, which is the same method the church has been using for centuries.

---

[1] *Back to School.* Performed by Rodney Dangerfield. Hollywood: CA: Paper Clip Productions, 1986. DVD.

Hebraic teaching methods are different. The teacher wants the students to challenge what they hear. It is through questioning that a student can learn. In addition, the teacher wants his/her students to excel to a point where the student becomes the teacher.

It is said that if two rabbis come together to discuss a passage of Scripture, the result will be at least ten different opinions. All points of view are acceptable as long as the points can be supported by biblical evidence. It is permissible and encourages students to have multiple opinions. There is a depth to God's Word, and God wants us to find all of His messages that are placed in the Scriptures.

Seeking the meaning of the Scriptures beyond the literal meaning is essential to fully understanding God's Word.[2] The Greek method of learning the Scriptures has prevailed over the centuries. One problem is that only the literal interpretation of Scripture was often viewed as valid, as prompted by Martin Luther's "sola literalis" meaning that only the literal interpretation of Scripture was valid. The Fundamentalist movements of today are based on the literal interpretation of the Scripture. Therefore, they do not believe that God placed any deeper, hidden, or secret meanings in the Word.

The students of the Scriptures who learn through Hebraic training and understanding have drawn a different conclusion. The Hebrew language itself leads to different interpretations because of the construction of

---

[2] Davis, Anne Kimball. *The Synoptic Gospels*. MP3. Albuquerque: NM: BibleInteract, 2012.

the language. The Hebraic method of Bible study opens up avenues of thought about God's revelations in the Scripture that may have never been considered. A question may be raised about the Scripture being studied for which there may not be an immediate answer. If so, it becomes the responsibility of the learners to uncover the meaning. Also, remember that multiple opinions about the meaning of Scripture are also acceptable if they can be supported by Scripture.

Methodology

The method employed is to use First Century Scripture study methods integrated with the customs and culture of Yeshua's day to examine the Hebrew and Christian Scriptures, thus gathering a deeper understanding by learning the Scriptures in the way the people of Yeshua's day did.

In a typical Rabbinic tradition, I had two study partners. Each one served a different function by looking at the research as I put it together. Rev. Dr. Robert Cook, D. Min., an ordained Elder in the United Methodist Church, has been a study partner in different areas of theology and church leadership. He became interested in Hebraic studies when I started sharing Zohar and Midrash with him. He also completed the entire Disciple program as a student and teacher. My second study partner is my wife, Sandra Koplitz, MS. Sandy and I took the instruction class on teaching the Disciple Bible study program and she takes part in the Zohar study group. Sandy is a licensed local pastor in the United Methodist Church.

The Process of Discovery

I have titled the method of analyzing a passage of Scripture in a Hebraic manner the "Process of Discovery." This method was developed by the author, bringing together the various areas of linguistic and cultural understanding. There are several sections to the process, and not all the sections apply to every passage of Scripture. The overall result of developing this process is to give the reader a framework into the ideas being presented.

The "Process of Discovery" starts with a Scripture passage. If the passage is in a poetic form, it is identified. Possible poetic techniques include parallelism, chiastic structures, and repetition. Formatting the passage in its poetic form allows the reader to visualize what the first century CE listener was hearing. The chiasms are labeled by their corresponding sections, for example: A, B, C, B', A'. Not all passages of the Scriptures have a poetic form.

The next step is to "question the narrative," which is accomplished by assuming the reader knows nothing about the passage. Therefore, the questions go from the simple to the complex. The next task is to identify any linguistic patterns. Linguistic patterns include, but are not limited to irony, simile, metaphor, symbolism, idioms, hyperbole, figurative language, personification, and allegory.

Any translation inconsistencies discovered between the English NASB version and either the Hebrew or Greek versions are identified. Sometimes a Hebrew or Greek word can be translated in more than one way. Inconsistencies also can be created by the translation committee, which may have used traditional language instead of the actual translation. The decision of the translation committee can be found in the Preface or Introduction to the Bible. Perhaps some inconsistencies were intentionally added to convey some deeper meaning, therefore the inconsistencies need to be examined.

Echoes of the Hebrew Scriptures in the Christian Scripture are identified. This occurs when a passage from the Hebrew Scripture is used in the Christian Scripture or when a Mitzvot is directly discussed in the Christian Scriptures.[3] In addition, echoes can be found when Torah (Genesis through Deuteronomy) passages are used in other Hebrew Bible books. Besides echoes, cross-references are listed. A cross reference is a reference to another verse in the Scripture which can assist the reader to understand the verse that is being read.

The names of people mentioned in the passage are listed. Many of the Hebrew names have meaning and may be associated with places or actions. Jewish parents used to name their children based on what they felt God had in

---

[3] Mitzvot are the 613 commandments found in the Torah that please God. There are positive and negative commandments. The list was first development by Maimonides. The full list can be found at: ttp://www.jewfaq.org/613.htm.

store for their child. An example of this is Abraham, whose original name was Abram, and was changed to mean eternal father (in this case Abram's name was changed by God to Abraham, showing a function he was to perform). When the Hebrew Bible gives names, many of the occurrences will show something special to the reader/listener. The same importance can hold true for the names of places. The time to travel between places can supply insight to the event.

Keywords are identified in a verse when they are important to an understanding of that passage. There are no rules for selecting the keywords. Searching for other occurrences of the keywords in Scripture in a concordance is necessary to understand how the word was being used; this must be done in either Hebrew or Greek, not in English. A classic Hebraic approach is to find the usage of a word in the Scripture by finding other verses that contain the word. The usage of a word, in its original language, is discovered by searching the Scripture in the biblical language. The verses that contain the word being researched are identified and a pattern for the usage of the word is discerned. Each verse is examined to see what the usage of the word is, which may reveal a pattern for the word's usage. For Hebrew words, the first usage of the word in the Scripture, especially if used in the Torah, is important. For the Greek words, the Christian Scriptures are used to determining the word usage in the Scripture. Sometimes finding the equivalent Greek word in the Septuagint and then analyzing its usage in Hebrew can be very helpful.

The Rules of Hillel for Bible understanding can be used when applicable. Hillel was a Torah scholar who lived shortly before Yeshua's day. Hillel developed several rules for Torah students to interpret the Scriptures which are referred to as halachic midrash. In several cases, these rules are helpful in the analysis of the Scripture.

After the linguistic analysis is complete, an examination of cultural implications will be examined. The culture is important because it is not specifically referenced in the biblical narratives as shown earlier.

From linguistic analysis and the cultural understanding, it is possible to get a deeper meaning of the Scripture beyond the literal meaning of the plaintext. That is what the listeners of Yeshua's time were doing. They put linguistics and the culture together without even having to contemplate it. They did it.

This will lead to a conclusion or a set of conclusions about what the passage is discussing. Most of the time, the Hebraic analysis leads to the desire for a deeper analysis in order to fully understand what Yeshua was discussing or what was happening to Him. Whatever the result, a new deeper understanding of the Scripture will be obtained.

The components of the Process of Discovery are:

      Linguistics Section

      Linguistic Structure of the Scripture

      Discussion

      Questioning the Passage

Main/Center Point

Verse Comparison on citations or proof text

Idioms

Metaphors

Symbols

Translation inconsistencies

People's names

Name of places

Word Study

Topics

Scripture cross references

Echoes

Rules of Hillel

Culture Section

Discussion

Questioning the passage culturally

Culture and Linguistics Section

Discussion

Only the sections that are applicable to each chapter are presented.

Malachi Chapter One

Malachi means "my angel, my messenger" or "my counselor." He lived during the Persian period when Judah was a part of the Persian Empire and administered by a governor under Persian rule. His prophecy was after the rebuilding of the Second Temple in Jerusalem. The sacrificial system had been restarted and Jews were beginning to return to the Promised Land. Many men had married foreign wives and were being unfaithful to the LORD. Malachi condemned the priests for growing careless in their priestly duties. The priests were allowing sacrifices of blemished and blind animals. This polluted the offerings to the LORD who required perfect sacrifices. The people in Judah became lax in their payments of tithes to the LORD. It is Malachi who predicts the arrival of John the Baptist who prepared the way for the Messiah Yeshua. Malachi's writing reignited the people to a more fervent and life dedicated to their religion and reverence for the LORD with true worship.[4]

---

[4] Errico, Rocco A., and George M. Lamsa. "Malachi Chapter One." In Aramaic Light on Ezekiel, Daniel, and the Minor Prophets: A Commentary Based on the Aramaic Language and Ancient Near Eastern Customs. Smyma, GA: Noohra Foundation, 2012.

Language

New American Standard 1995	Hebrew	Septuagint
[1] The oracle of the word of the LORD to Israel through Malachi. [2] "I have loved you," says the LORD. But you say, "How have You loved us?" "*Was* not Esau Jacob's brother?" declares the LORD. "Yet I have loved Jacob; [3] but I have hated Esau, and I have	מַשָּׂא [WTT] דְּבַר־יְהוָה אֶל־יִשְׂרָאֵל בְּיַד מַלְאָכִי׃ [2] אָהַבְתִּי אֶתְכֶם אָמַר יְהוָה וַאֲמַרְתֶּם בַּמָּה אֲהַבְתָּנוּ הֲלוֹא־אָח עֵשָׂו לְיַעֲקֹב נְאֻם־יְהוָה וָאֹהַב אֶת־יַעֲקֹב׃ [3] וְאֶת־עֵשָׂו שָׂנֵאתִי וָאָשִׂים אֶת־הָרָיו שְׁמָמָה וְאֶת־נַחֲלָתוֹ לְתַנּוֹת מִדְבָּר׃	The burden of the word of the Lord to Israel by the hand of his messenger. Lay *it*, I pray you, to heart. [2] I have loved you, saith the Lord. And ye said, Wherein hast thou loved us? Was not Esau Jacob's brother? saith the Lord: yet I loved Jacob, [3] and hated Esau and laid waste his borders, and made his heritage as

Column 1 (English)

made his mountains a desolation and *appointed* his inheritance for the jackals of the wilderness."

4 Though Edom says, "We have been beaten down, but we will return and build up the ruins"; thus says the LORD of hosts, "They may build, but I will tear down; and *men* will call them the wicked territory, and the people toward whom

Column 2 (Hebrew)

4 כִּי־תֹאמַר אֱדוֹם רֻשַּׁשְׁנוּ וְנָשׁוּב וְנִבְנֶה חֳרָבוֹת כֹּה אָמַר יְהוָה צְבָאוֹת הֵמָּה יִבְנוּ וַאֲנִי אֶהֱרוֹס וְקָרְאוּ לָהֶם גְּבוּל רִשְׁעָה וְהָעָם אֲשֶׁר־זָעַם יְהוָה עַד־עוֹלָם: 5 וְעֵינֵיכֶם תִּרְאֶינָה וְאַתֶּם תֹּאמְרוּ יִגְדַּל יְהוָה מֵעַל לִגְבוּל יִשְׂרָאֵל: 6 בֵּן יְכַבֵּד אָב וְעֶבֶד אֲדֹנָיו וְאִם־אָב אָנִי אַיֵּה כְבוֹדִי וְאִם־

Column 3 (English)

dwellings of the wilderness?

4 Because one will say, Idumea has been overthrown, but let us return and rebuild the desolate places; thus saith the Lord Almighty, They shall build, but I will throw down; and they shall be called The borders of wickedness, and, The people against whom the Lord has set himself for ever.

5 And your eyes shall see,

the LORD is indignant forever."

5 Your eyes will see this and you will say, "The LORD be magnified beyond the border of Israel!"

6 "'A son honors *his* father, and a servant his master. Then if I am a father, where is My honor? And if I am a master, where is My respect?' says the LORD of hosts to you, O priests who despise My name. But

אֲדוֹנִים אָנִי אַיֵּה מוֹרָאִי אָמַר יְהוָה צְבָאוֹת לָכֶם הַכֹּהֲנִים בּוֹזֵי שְׁמִי וַאֲמַרְתֶּם בַּמֶּה בָזִינוּ אֶת־שְׁמֶךָ: 7 מַגִּישִׁים עַל־מִזְבְּחִי לֶחֶם מְגֹאָל וַאֲמַרְתֶּם בַּמֶּה גֵאַלְנוּךָ בֶּאֱמָרְכֶם שֻׁלְחַן יְהוָה נִבְזֶה הוּא: 8 וְכִי־תַגִּשׁוּן עִוֵּר לִזְבֹּחַ אֵין רָע וְכִי תַגִּישׁוּ פִּסֵּחַ וְחֹלֶה אֵין רָע הַקְרִיבֵהוּ נָא לְפֶחָתֶךָ הֲיִרְצְךָ אוֹ הֲיִשָּׂא פָנֶיךָ

and ye shall say, The Lord has been magnified upon the borders of Israel.

6 A son honours *his* father, and a servant his master: if then I am a father, where is mine honour? and if I am a master, where is my fear? saith the Lord Almighty. Ye the priests are they that despise my name: yet ye said, Wherein have we despised thy name?

you say, 'How have we despised Your name?'
7 "*You* are presenting defiled food upon My altar. But you say, 'How have we defiled You?' In that you say, 'The table of the LORD is to be despised.'
8 "But when you present the blind for sacrifice, is it not evil? And when you present the lame and sick, is it not evil? Why not offer it to your governor?

אָמַר יְהֹוָה צְבָאֽוֹת׃ 9 וְעַתָּה חַלּוּ־נָא פְנֵי־אֵל וִיחׇנֵּנוּ מִיֶּדְכֶם הָיְתָה זֹּאת הֲיִשָּׂא מִכֶּם פָּנִים אָמַר יְהֹוָה צְבָאֽוֹת׃ 10 מִי גַם־בָּכֶם וְיִסְגֹּר דְּלָתַיִם וְלֹא־תָאִירוּ מִזְבְּחִי חִנָּם אֵֽין־לִי חֵפֶץ בָּכֶם אָמַר יְהֹוָה צְבָאוֹת וּמִנְחָה לֹא־אֶרְצֶה מִיֶּדְכֶֽם׃ 11 כִּי מִמִּזְרַח־שֶׁמֶשׁ וְעַד־מְבוֹאוֹ גָּדוֹל

7 In that ye bring to mine altar polluted bread; and ye said, Wherein have ye polluted it? In that ye say, The table of the Lord is polluted, and that which was set thereon ye have despised.
8 For if ye bring a blind *victim* for sacrifices, *is it* not evil? and if ye bring the lame or the sick, *is it* not evil? offer it now to thy ruler, *and see* if he will receive thee, if he will accept thy person, saith

Would he be pleased with you? Or would he receive you kindly?" says the LORD of hosts.

9 "But now will you not entreat God's favor, that He may be gracious to us? With such an offering on your part, will He receive any of you kindly?" says the LORD of hosts.

10 "Oh that there were one among you who would shut the gates, that you might not

שְׁמִי בַּגּוֹיִם וּבְכָל־מָקוֹם מֻקְטָר מֻגָּשׁ לִשְׁמִי וּמִנְחָה טְהוֹרָה כִּי־ גָדוֹל שְׁמִי בַּגּוֹיִם אָמַר יְהוָה צְבָאוֹת: 12 וְאַתֶּם מְחַלְּלִים אוֹתוֹ בֶּאֱמָרְכֶם שֻׁלְחַן אֲדֹנָי מְגֹאָל הוּא וְנִיבוֹ נִבְזֶה אָכְלוֹ: 13 וַאֲמַרְתֶּם הִנֵּה מַתְּלָאָה וְהִפַּחְתֶּם אוֹתוֹ אָמַר יְהוָה צְבָאוֹת וַהֲבֵאתֶם גָּזוּל וְאֶת־ הַפִּסֵּחַ

the Lord Almighty.

9 And now intreat the face of your God, and make supplication to him. These things have been done by your hands; shall I accept you? saith the Lord Almighty.

10 Because even among you the doors shall be shut, and *one* will not kindle *the fire of* mine altar for nothing, I have no pleasure in you, saith the Lord Almighty, and I will not accept a

uselessly kindle *fire on* My altar! I am not pleased with you," says the LORD of hosts, "nor will I accept an offering from you. [11] "For from the rising of the sun even to its setting, My name *will be* great among the nations, and in every place incense is going to be offered to My name, and a grain offering *that is* pure; for My name *will be* great among the

וְאֶת־הַחוֹלֶה וַהֲבֵאתֶם אֶת־הַמִּנְחָה הַאֶרְצֶה אוֹתָהּ מִיֶּדְכֶם אָמַר יְהוָה: ס [14] וְאָרוּר נוֹכֵל וְיֵשׁ בְּעֶדְרוֹ זָכָר וְנֹדֵר וְזֹבֵחַ מָשְׁחָת לַאדֹנָי כִּי מֶלֶךְ גָּדוֹל אָנִי אָמַר יְהוָה צְבָאוֹת וּשְׁמִי נוֹרָא בַגּוֹיִם:

sacrifice at your hands. [11] For from the rising of the sun even to the going down *thereof* my name has been glorified among the Gentiles; and in every place incense is offered to my name, and a pure offering: for my name is great among the Gentiles, saith the Lord Almighty. [12] But ye profane it, in that ye say, The table of the Lord is polluted, and his meats set

nations," says the LORD of hosts. 12 "But you are profaning it, in that you say, 'The table of the Lord is defiled, and as for its fruit, its food is to be despised.' 13 "You also say, 'My, how tiresome it is!' And you disdainfully sniff at it," says the LORD of hosts, "and you bring what was taken by robbery and *what is* lame or sick; so you bring the offering!		thereon are despised. 13 And ye said, These *services* are troublesome: therefore I have utterly rejected them with scorn, saith the Lord Almighty: and ye brought in torn victims, and lame, and sick: if then ye should bring an offering, shall I accept them at your hands? saith the Lord Almighty. 14 And cursed *is the man* who had the power, and possessed a male in his flock, and

Should I receive that from your hand?" says the LORD. [14] "But cursed be the swindler who has a male in his flock and vows it, but sacrifices a blemished animal to the Lord, for I am a great King," says the LORD of hosts, "and My name is feared among the nations."		whose vow is upon him, and who sacrifices a corrupt thing to the Lord: for I am a great King, saith the Lord Almighty, and my name is glorious among the nations.

Process of Discovery

Linguistics Section

Linguistic Structure

[Introduction] [1] The oracle of the word of the LORD to Israel through Malachi.

A [2] **"I have loved you,"** says the LORD. But you say, "How have You loved us?" "*Was* not Esau Jacob's brother?" declares the LORD. "Yet I have loved Jacob; [3] but I have hated Esau, and I have made his mountains a desolation and *appointed* his inheritance for the jackals of the wilderness." [4] Though Edom says, "We have been beaten down, but we will return and build up the ruins"; thus says the LORD of hosts, "They may build, but I will tear down; and *men* will call them the wicked territory, and the people toward whom the LORD is indignant forever."

B' [5] Your eyes will see this and you will say, **"The LORD be magnified beyond the border of Israel!"** [6] "'A son honors *his* father, and a servant his master. Then if I am a father, where is My honor? And if I am a master, where is My respect?' says the

LORD of hosts to you, O priests who despise My name. But you say, 'How have we despised Your name?

C [7] "***You*** **are presenting defiled food upon My altar**. But you say, 'How have we defiled You?' In that you say, 'The table of the LORD is to be despised.' [8] "But when you present the blind for sacrifice, is it not evil? And when you present the lame and sick, is it not evil? Why not offer it to your governor? Would he be pleased with you? Or would he receive you kindly?" says the LORD of hosts.

A' [9] "But now will you not entreat **God's favor**, that He may be gracious to us? With such an offering on your part, will He receive any of you kindly?" says the LORD of hosts. [10] "Oh that there were one among you who would shut the gates, that you might not uselessly kindle *fire on* My altar! I am not pleased with you," says the LORD of hosts, "nor will I accept an offering from you.

B' [11] "For from the rising of the sun even to its setting, **My name *will be* great among the nations**, and in every place incense is going to be offered to My name, and a grain offering *that is* pure; for My name *will be* **great among the nations**," says the LORD of hosts.

> **C'** [12] **"But you are profaning it, in that you say**, 'The table of the Lord is defiled, and as for its fruit, its food is to be despised.'[13] "You also say, 'My, how tiresome it is!' And you disdainfully sniff at it," says the LORD of hosts, "and you bring what was taken by robbery and *what is* lame or sick; so you bring the offering! Should I receive that from your hand?" says the LORD.

Key to the chiasm: A: The love of the LORD. B: The name of the LORD is great among the nations. C: Polluted altar.[5]

[14] "But cursed be the swindler who has a male in his flock and vows it, but sacrifices a blemished animal to the Lord, for I am a great King," says the LORD of hosts, "and My name is feared among the nations."

---

[5] "Literary Structure (chiasm, Chiasmus) of Book of Malachi." Literary Structure (chiasm, Chiasmus) of Each Pericopes of Book of Malachi. Accessed March 18, 2017. (Malachi Chiasms n.d.).

Discussion

The chapter consists of one A-B-C-A'-B'-C' chiasm. Verse 14 is a conclusion of the chiasm.

Questioning the Passage

1. How does Esau fit into the description the LORD is giving? (v. 1 through 4)

   The people of Judah are reminded that Esau and Jacob were twin brothers, and the LORD showed favor to Jacob and loved Jacob and his children more than He loved Esau. It was the descendants of Jacob who received the promises that God gave to Abraham. The constant destruction and rebuilding of Edom tells us that the protection the LORD gave to Jacob's children was not offered to Edom.

Subsequently, throughout history, the nation of Esau (Edom) experienced invasion, destruction, and rebuilding many times. Jacob's children are told this to remind them they had the protection and love of the LORD and they were not showing their love back to the LORD.

2. How has the LORD been despised as stated in verse 5 & 6?

Sometimes Edom was in ruins, destroyed by enemies, while Israel was protected by the LORD and the people prospered. All the LORD asked from His people was to follow the Laws in the Torah. The people despised the LORD by violating His Laws.

3. What was the problem with the sacrifices in that day? (v. 7 & 8)

    The people were bringing imperfect animals for their sacrifice. This is a violation of the sacrifice laws the LORD gave to Israel. Only perfect animals were to be sacrificed to the LORD.

4. How does the governor fit in with the words of defiled sacrifices? (v. 7 & 8)

    The LORD was saying to the priests that the sacrifices they were offering to the LORD would not have been offered to the governor of Judea. The priests were offering sub-standard animals to the LORD who should have been receiving the best the people had. The offering to their governor was better than those given to the LORD. The future of the people was in the LORD's hand and not that of the governor's.

5. What does the sacrifice of a male of the flock mean? (v. 14)

    Malachi is offering a curse to anyone who has a perfect male ram in his flock and brings an imperfect one for a sacrifice for sin.

Main/Center Point

The people have returned from Exile in Babylon. The Temple has been rebuilt in Jerusalem. The people insulted the LORD because instead of bringing their best offering for the necessary sacrifices; they brought their worst. The LORD told the people that He chose them and loved them. The LORD protected them while He allowed their cousin Edom to suffer. The people should have respected the love of the LORD.

Symbols

1. What are the gates that are mentioned in verse ten?

   The gates are the doors to the Temple. The LORD is saying through Malachi that He wished that a faithful priest would stop the imperfect sacrifices. The closing of the gates symbolized the stopping of the sacrifices. The LORD wanted the impure sacrifice to stop at all costs.[6]

---

[6] Scherman, Nosson, Meir Zlotowitz, Sheah Brander, and Menachem Davis. "Micah." In The Prophets: The Later Prophets with a Commentary Anthologized from the Rabbinic Writings. Brooklyn, NY: Mesorah Publications, 2013. p. 491.

2. What is the symbolism of fire on the altar? (v. 10)

The fire on the altar was there for the sacrifice. The fatty parts of the animal were placed on the altar and the smell would be a pleasing aroma to the LORD. But since the LORD wanted the impure sacrifices to stop, the fire on the altar was ended. The LORD was saying "stop the sacrifices." The LORD would rather not have any sacrifices than the ones that were being offered by the people in Malachi's time. By offering imperfect sacrifices, the people were saying to the LORD that He was not the most important part of their lives. It is like having a meal then offering the table scraps to the LORD. Showing your trust and faith in the LORD means offering your best. Today, when followers of Yeshua offer what is left in your checking accounts to the church's tithe, not the first check but the last check, they are doing the same thing as offering imperfect sacrifices.

People's names

1. מַלְאָכִי *Malaki* **Meaning:** 'my messenger,' an Israeli prophet
2. יַעֲקֹב *Yaaqob* **Meaning:** a son of Isaac, also his descendants
3. עֵשָׂו *Esav* **Meaning:** oldest son of Isaac

Scripture cross references

Verse 1   Isa 13:1; Nah 1:1; Hab 1:1; Zec 9:1

Verse 2   Deu 4:37; Deu 7:8; Deu 23:5; Isa 41:8, Isa 41:9; Jer 31:3; Joh 15:12; Rom 9:13

Verse 3   Jer 49:10, Jer 49:16-18; Eze 35:3, Eze 35:4, 7, 8, 15

Verse 5   Psa 35:27; Mic 5:4

Verse 6   Exo 20:12; Pro 30:11, Pro 30:17; Deu 1:31; Isa 1:2; Jer 3:4; Mal 2:10; Zep 3:4

Verse 8   Lev 22:22; Deu 15:21; Hag 1:1

Verse 9   Jer 27:18; Joe 2:12-14; Amo 5:22

Verse 14   Act 5:1-4; Lev 22:18-20; Zec 14:9; Zep 2:11

Thoughts

The warning that the LORD gave to Malachi to give to the people of Judah is applicable today. Do you give your best to the LORD? The LORD asks for a tithing, 10% of income. There are many people today who rationalize a tithe to 1.5% or less of their income because they envision tithing as "paying for the worship service" and not being a gift to God. There are many people today who spend more money on their cable bills than they do giving to the LORD. To give less than 10% is to insult the LORD by accepting the love of the LORD but not being willing to do what the LORD asks. There will be many people who will reach judgment day and will be judged on tithing. Many will fail the test. In churches today, pastors are told by their congregations not to discuss money. The people feel the pastor has no right to tell them what the Bible says about tithing. The message is simple. Give to the LORD that which is the LORD's. These are the words of Yeshua, our Messiah, Lord and Savior.

Malachi Chapter Two

Language

New American Standard 1995	Hebrew	Septuagint
1 "And now this commandment is for you, O priests. 2 "If you do not listen, and if you do not take it to heart to give honor to My name," says the LORD of hosts, "then I will send the curse upon you and I will curse your blessings; and indeed, I have cursed	^{WTT} וְעַתָּה אֲלֵיכֶם הַמִּצְוָה הַזֹּאת הַכֹּהֲנִים: ² אִם־לֹא תִשְׁמְעוּ וְאִם־לֹא תָשִׂימוּ עַל־לֵב לָתֵת כָּבוֹד לִשְׁמִי אָמַר יְהוָה צְבָאוֹת וְשִׁלַּחְתִּי בָכֶם אֶת־הַמְּאֵרָה וְאָרוֹתִי	And now, O priests, this commandment is to you. ² If ye will not hearken, and if ye will not lay *it* to heart, to give glory to my name, saith the Lord Almighty, then I will send forth the curse upon you, and I will bring a curse upon your blessing: yea, I will curse it, and I will scatter your blessing, and it shall not

them *already*, because you are not taking *it* to heart. 3 "Behold, I am going to rebuke your offspring, and I will spread refuse on your faces, the refuse of your feasts; and you will be taken away with it. 4 "Then you will know that I have sent this commandment to you, that My covenant may continue with Levi," says the LORD of hosts. 5 "My covenant with him was *one of* life and peace,	אֶת־בִּרְכוֹתֵיכֶם וְגַם אָרוֹתִיהָ כִּי אֵינְכֶם שָׂמִים עַל־לֵב: 3 הִנְנִי גֹעֵר לָכֶם אֶת־הַזֶּרַע וְזֵרִיתִי פֶרֶשׁ עַל־פְּנֵיכֶם פֶּרֶשׁ חַגֵּיכֶם וְנָשָׂא אֶתְכֶם אֵלָיו: 4 וִידַעְתֶּם כִּי שִׁלַּחְתִּי אֲלֵיכֶם אֵת הַמִּצְוָה הַזֹּאת לִהְיוֹת בְּרִיתִי	exist among you, because ye lay not this to heart. 3 Behold, I turn my back upon you, and I will scatter dung upon your faces, the dung of your feasts, and I will carry you away at the same time. 4 And ye shall know that I have sent this commandment to you, that my covenant might be with the sons of Levi, saith the Lord Almighty. 5 My covenant of life and peace was with him, and I gave *it* him that he might

and I gave them to him *as an object of* reverence; so he revered Me and stood in awe of My name.

6 "True instruction was in his mouth and unrighteousnes s was not found on his lips; he walked with Me in peace and uprightness, and he turned many back from iniquity.

7 "For the lips of a priest should preserve knowledge, and men should seek instruction from his mouth; for he is

אֶת־לָֽוֹ
אָמַר
יְהוָה
צְבָאֽוֹת:
5 בְּרִיתִי
הָיְתָה
אִתּוֹ
הַֽחַיִּים
וְהַשָּׁלוֹם
וָאֶתְּנֵֽם־לוֹ
מוֹרָא
וַיִּֽירָאֵנִי
וּמִפְּנֵי
שְׁמִי נִחַת
הֽוּא:
6 תּוֹרַת
אֱמֶת
הָיְתָה
בְּפִיהוּ
וְעַוְלָה
לֹא־נִמְצָא
בִשְׂפָתָיו
בְּשָׁלוֹם
וּבְמִישׁוֹר
הָלַךְ אִתִּי
וְרַבִּים
הֵשִׁיב
מֵעָוֺֽן:

reverently fear me, and that he might be awe-struck at my name.

6 The law of truth was in his mouth, and iniquity was not found in his lips: he walked before me directing *his way* in peace, and he turned many from unrighteousness.

7 For the priest's lips should keep knowledge, and they should seek the law at his mouth: for he is the messenger of the Lord Almighty.

the messenger of the LORD of hosts. 8 "But as for you, you have turned aside from the way; you have caused many to stumble by the instruction; you have corrupted the covenant of Levi," says the LORD of hosts. 9 "So I also have made you despised and abased before all the people, just as you are not keeping My ways but are showing partiality in the instruction. 10 "Do we not all have one

7 כִּי־שִׂפְתֵי כֹהֵן יִשְׁמְרוּ־דַעַת וְתוֹרָה יְבַקְשׁוּ מִפִּיהוּ כִּי מַלְאַךְ יְהוָה־צְבָאוֹת הוּא׃ 8 וְאַתֶּם סַרְתֶּם מִן־הַדֶּרֶךְ הִכְשַׁלְתֶּם רַבִּים בַּתּוֹרָה שִׁחַתֶּם בְּרִית הַלֵּוִי אָמַר יְהוָה צְבָאוֹת׃ 9 וְגַם־אֲנִי נָתַתִּי אֶתְכֶם נִבְזִים וּשְׁפָלִים

8 But ye have turned aside from the way, and caused many to fail in *following* the law: ye have corrupted the covenant of Levi, saith the Lord Almighty. 9 And I have made you despised and cast out among all the people, because ye have not kept my ways, but have been partial in the law. 10 Have ye not all one father? Did not one God create you? why have ye forsaken every man his brother, to profane the

father? Has not one God created us? Why do we deal treacherously each against his brother so as to profane the covenant of our fathers?

11 "Judah has dealt treacherously, and an abomination has been committed in Israel and in Jerusalem; for Judah has profaned the sanctuary of the LORD which He loves and has married the daughter of a foreign god.

12 "*As* for the man who does

לְכָל־הָעָם כְּפִי אֲשֶׁר אֵינְכֶם שֹׁמְרִים אֶת־דְּרָכַי וְנֹשְׂאִים פָּנִים בַּתּוֹרָה: פ

10 הֲלוֹא אָב אֶחָד לְכֻלָּנוּ הֲלוֹא אֵל אֶחָד בְּרָאָנוּ מַדּוּעַ נִבְגַּד אִישׁ בְּאָחִיו לְחַלֵּל בְּרִית אֲבֹתֵינוּ:

11 בָּגְדָה יְהוּדָה וְתוֹעֵבָה נֶעֶשְׂתָה בְיִשְׂרָאֵל וּבִירוּשָׁלַם כִּי

covenant of your fathers?

11 Juda has been forsaken, and an abomination has been committed in Israel and in Jerusalem; for Juda has profaned the holy things of the Lord, which he delighted in, and has gone after other gods.

12 The Lord will utterly destroy the man that does these things, until he be even cast down from out of the tabernacles of Jacob, and from among them that offer

this, may the LORD cut off from the tents of Jacob *everyone* who awakes and answers, or who presents an offering to the LORD of hosts.

13 "This is another thing you do: you cover the altar of the LORD with tears, with weeping and with groaning, because He no longer regards the offering or accepts *it with* favor from your hand.

14 "Yet you say, 'For what reason?' Because the LORD has

חִלֵּל
יְהוּדָ֖ה
קֹ֑דֶשׁ
יְהוָה֙
אֲשֶׁ֣ר
אָהֵ֔ב
וּבָעַ֖ל
בַּת־אֵ֥ל
נֵכָֽר׃
12 יַכְרֵ֨ת
יְהֹוָ֜ה
לָאִ֨ישׁ
אֲשֶׁ֤ר
יַעֲשֶׂ֙נָּה֙
עֵ֣ר וְעֹנֶ֔ה
מֵאָהֳלֵ֖י
יַעֲקֹ֑ב
וּמַגִּ֥ישׁ
מִנְחָ֖ה
לַיהוָ֥ה
צְבָאֽוֹת׃ פ
13 וְזֹאת֙
שֵׁנִ֣ית
תַּעֲשׂ֔וּ
כַּסּ֤וֹת
דִּמְעָה֙
אֶת־
מִזְבַּ֣ח

sacrifice to the Lord Almighty.

13 And these things which I hated, ye did: ye covered with tears the altar of the Lord, and with weeping and groaning because of troubles: *is it* meet *for me* to have respect to your sacrifice, or to receive *anything* from your hands *as* welcome?

14 Yet ye said, Wherefore? Because the Lord has borne witness between thee and the wife of thy youth, whom thou has forsaken, and *yet*

been a witness between you and the wife of your youth, against whom you have dealt treacherously, though she is your companion and your wife by covenant.

15 "But not one has done *so* who has a remnant of the Spirit. And what did *that* one *do* while he was seeking a godly offspring? Take heed then to your spirit, and let no one deal treacherously against the wife of your youth.

יְהוָֹה בְּכִי וַאֲנָקָה מֵאֵין עוֹד פְּנוֹת אֶל־הַמִּנְחָה וְלָקַחַת רָצוֹן מִיֶּדְכֶם:

14 וַאֲמַרְתֶּם עַל־מֶה עַל כִּי־יְהוָֹה הֵעִיד בֵּינְךָ וּבֵין אֵשֶׁת נְעוּרֶיךָ אֲשֶׁר אַתָּה בָּגַדְתָּה בָּהּ וְהִיא חֲבֶרְתְּךָ וְאֵשֶׁת בְּרִיתֶךָ:

15 וְלֹא־אֶחָד עָשָׂה וּשְׁאָר

she was thy partner, and the wife of thy covenant.

15 And did he not do well? and *there was* the residue of his spirit. But ye said, What does God seek but a seed? But take ye heed to your spirit, and forsake not the wife of thy youth.

16 But if thou shouldest hate *thy wife* and put her away, saith the Lord God of Israel, then ungodliness shall cover thy thoughts, saith the Lord Almighty: therefore take

16 "For I hate divorce," says the LORD, the God of Israel, "and him who covers his garment with wrong," says the LORD of hosts. "So take heed to your spirit, that you do not deal treacherously." 17 You have wearied the LORD with your words. Yet you say, "How have we wearied *Him*?" In that you say, "Everyone who does evil is good in the sight of the LORD, and He delights in them," or,	רֹוּחַ לֹו וּמָה הָאֶחָד מְבַקֵּשׁ זֶרַע אֱלֹהִים וְנִשְׁמַרְתֶּם בְּרוּחֲכֶם וּבְאֵשֶׁת נְעוּרֶיךָ אַל־יִבְגָּד: 16 כִּי־שָׂנֵא שַׁלַּח אָמַר יְהוָה אֱלֹהֵי יִשְׂרָאֵל וְכִסָּה חָמָס עַל־לְבוּשׁו אָמַר יְהוָה צְבָאֹות וְנִשְׁמַרְתֶּם בְּרוּחֲכֶם	ye heed to your spirit, and forsake *them* not, 17 ye that have provoked God with your words. But ye said, Wherein have we provoked him? In that ye say, Every one that does evil is a pleasing *object* in the sight of the Lord, and he takes pleasure in such; and where is the God of justice?

"Where is the God of justice?"	וְלֹא תִבְגֹּדוּ׃ ס 17 הוֹגַעְתֶּם יְהוָה֙ בְּדִבְרֵיכֶ֔ם וַאֲמַרְתֶּ֖ם בַּמָּ֣ה הוֹגָ֑עְנוּ בֶּאֱמָרְכֶ֗ם כָּל־עֹ֨שֵׂה רָ֜ע ט֣וֹב ׀ בְּעֵינֵ֣י יְהוָ֗ה וּבָהֶם֙ ה֣וּא חָפֵ֔ץ א֥וֹ אַיֵּ֖ה אֱלֹהֵ֥י הַמִּשְׁפָּֽט׃	

Process of Discovery

Linguistics Section

Linguistic Structure

A [1] "And now **this commandment is for you**, O priests. [2] "If you do not listen, and if you do not take it to heart to give honor to My name," says the LORD of hosts, "then I will send the curse upon you and I will curse your blessings; and indeed, I have cursed them *already*, because you are not taking *it* to heart.

B [3] "Behold, I am going to rebuke your offspring, and I will spread refuse on your faces, the refuse of your feasts; and you will be taken away with it.

A' [4] "Then you will know that I have sent **this commandment to you**, that My covenant may continue with Levi," says the LORD of hosts. [5] "My covenant with him was *one of* life and peace, and I gave them to him *as an object of* reverence; so he revered Me and stood in awe of My name.

R1 [6] "True instruction was in his mouth and unrighteousness was not found on his lips; he walked with Me in peace and uprightness, and he turned many back from iniquity.

R2 [7] "For the lips of a priest should preserve knowledge, and men should seek instruction from his mouth; for he is the messenger of the LORD of hosts.

R3 [8] "But as for you, you have turned aside from the way; you have caused many to stumble by the instruction; you have corrupted the covenant of Levi," says the LORD of hosts. [9] "So I also have made you despised and abased before all the people, just as you are not keeping My ways but are showing partiality in the instruction. [Author's note: R1, R2, R3 are connected by subject]

A [10] "Do we not all have one father? Has not one God created us? **Why do we deal treacherously** each against his brother so as to profane the covenant of our fathers? [11] "Judah has dealt treacherously, and an abomination has been committed in Israel and in Jerusalem; for Judah has profaned the sanctuary of the LORD which He loves and has married the daughter of a foreign god.

B [12] "*As* for the man who does this, may the LORD cut off from the tents of Jacob *everyone* who awakes and answers, or who presents an offering to the LORD of hosts. [13] "This is another thing you do: you cover the altar of the LORD with tears, with weeping and with groaning, because He no longer regards the offering or accepts *it with* favor from your hand.

A' [14] "Yet you say, 'For what reason?' Because the LORD has been a witness between you and the wife of your youth, against **whom you have dealt treacherously**, though she is your companion and your wife by covenant. [15] "But not one has done *so* who has a remnant of the Spirit. And what did *that* one *do* while he was seeking a godly offspring? Take heed then to your spirit, and let no one deal treacherously against the wife of your youth. [16] "For I hate divorce," says the LORD, the God of Israel, "and him who covers his garment with wrong," says the LORD of hosts. "So take heed to your spirit, that you do not deal treacherously."

[closing statement] [17] You have wearied the LORD with your words. Yet you say, "How have we wearied *Him*?" In that you say, "Everyone who does evil is good in the sight of the LORD, and He delights in them," or, "Where is the God of justice?"

Discussion

This chapter comprises two A-B-A' chiasms which surround a set of three repetitive sections. The repetitions are based on the subject and because they are repetitive, they emphasize a point the LORD was offering.

The passage is directed at the priests of Israel and Judah. The LORD had entrusted them with the safety and security of the people. Instead of ensuring that they followed the ways of the LORD, the priests allowed the Baal and other worship practices to invade. The LORD, here, is holding the Levites responsible for, at least, some of the iniquities of the people.

Questioning the Passage

1. What was the curse of the LORD to the priests? (v. 2)

    There is no indication of what the curse from the LORD would be. Certainly, the blessings that the LORD had been sending to the priests would be discontinued.

2. Why would the LORD threaten to curse the priests in the future then turn around and say that He already cursed them? (v. 2)

    Rashi[7] said that the LORD knew the priests were not going to change their

---

[7] French commentator on Bible and Talmud; born at Troyes in 1040; died there July 13, 1105. His fame has made him the subject of many legends. Source: Liber, Morris, and M. Seligsohn. "Rashi." In Jewish Encyclopedia, by Joseph Jacobos. Seattle:WA: Funk and Wagnalls, 1906.

wicked ways, thus the LORD had the curses already in place ("ready to go").[8]

3. Why in verse one does Malachi says "priests" and in verse four change to "Levi?" (v. 4)

Metzudos, the Sage, claims that this verse has to do with the covenant that God made with Aaron that he and his descendants would maintain control over the priesthood. The change in language is to remind the priests that the original covenant which put them in charge was a covenant with Aaron.[9]

---

[8] Scherman, Nosson, Meir Zlotowitz, Sheah Brander, and Menachem Davis. "Micah." In The Prophets: The Later Prophets with a Commentary Anthologized from the Rabbinic Writings. Brooklyn, NY: Mesorah Publications, 2013. p. 493.
[9] IBID. P. 295.

4. What is true instruction? (v. 8)

   True instruction can be found in the Torah.

5. What is the covenant of Levi? (v. 8)

   The covenant is well explained in this article by Howell Jones.

THE COVENANT WITH LEVI

"We have referred to the events recorded in Exodus 32 and Numbers 25 in connection with this covenant. The first occurred at the foot of Sinai soon after the deliverance from Egypt, and the other in the plains of Moab, just as Israel was about to enter into the Promised Land. While Exodus 32 is, in our view, more suitable as the occasion, when the covenant was made because it involved the whole tribe of Levi, it is most important to note that both passages record a rebellion against God which manifested itself in idolatry and immorality. The first was associated with the episode of the Golden Calf and the other with the Baal of Peor.

The covenant with Levi was therefore an engagement made by the Lord in desperate circumstances. On each occasion, the Sinaitic covenant which had constituted the tribes of Israel as the people of God was being under-mined and openly flouted by the defection of the priests. Consequently, the transfer to Levi of the responsibility to teach and apply covenant law was intended not only to reform the people but also to preserve the theocracy.

Malachi saw this declension in the wilderness after deliverance from Egypt as repeating itself among those who had returned from exile in Babylon. He therefore spoke of how the covenant with Levi had been violated (2:8). But the history of God's redemptive purpose was continuing, and so he predicted that God would validate the covenant once more (2:4). This is all very relevant to what has happened to the church and its ministry of late, and is happening in our own day."[10]

6. Who is married to the daughter of a foreign God? (v. 11)

Malachi is scolding the men of his day because they were marrying non-Jewish women. The daughter of a foreign God are the non-Jewish women. The LORD through Malachi was giving the priests and example of how they were not helping the people to follow the LORD's Law. By the priests allowing these outside the faith marriage, they were permitting the people to sin.

---

[10] Jones, Howell. "Remembering a Forgotten Covenant." Westminster Seminary California. Accessed March 28, 2017. (Jones n.d.).

7. What is the symbolism of covering the altar of the LORD with tears? (v. 13)

The sin is the men not being faithful to the LORD. Rashi explains that the Jewish wives of these men are weeping because of this sin. Their weeping is so strong that it metaphorically covers the altar of the LORD. "The tears of the women attest to the evil of their husbands and encouraging the LORD not to accept their offerings.[11] It sounds like polygamy with a Jewish wife and additional gentile wives was being practiced.

---

[11] Scherman, Nosson, Meir Zlotowitz, Sheah Brander, and Menachem Davis. "Micah." In The Prophets: The Later Prophets with a Commentary Anthologized from the Rabbinic Writings. Brooklyn, NY: Mesorah Publications, 2013. p. 499.

8. What is the allegorical meaning of verse fourteen?

The LORD sees how the men of Judah have been treating their wives. If the men are breaking the Laws of the LORD, then they could easily cheat on their wives with the local Gentile women. The "wife of your youth" reminds the men that they married their Jewish wives while in their youth. Even though these were arranged marriages, the men were expected to learn to love their wives and to treat them properly. Remember, they had arranged marriages. They then married gentile women as they got older.

9. What does "covers injustice with his garment with violence" mean? (v. 16)

Rashi explains Malachi states that a man who hates his wife should divorce her, for her to find a husband who will love her. In addition, the man would find a woman more to his taste. There was much debate about this verse among the Sages. The LORD is not in favor of "no-fault" divorce. Since the LORD puts people together, the LORD is not eager to see them divorced. It is against the Law of the LORD to divorce your wife without compelling reasons.[12]

Main/Center Point

Malachi calls out the sin of Jewish men marrying non-Jewish women.

____

[12] IBID. p 501.

Symbols

1. What is the symbolism of spreading refuse on the faces of the priests? (v. 3)

   According to the Targum of Malachi, the refuse is referring to the iniquities of the priests. The LORD was going to show them their iniquities, directly in their faces.

2. What is the symbolism of spreading refuse of the feasts? (v. 3)

   The feasts are when the largest number of offerings came to the LORD. When the feasts occurred, the LORD was going to reject the offerings of the people and rub the rejection upon their faces. No matter what kind of offering the people brought into the LORD, He would not accept it.[13]

Culture Section

Questioning the passage

1. What does "spreading refuse (dung) on the face" mean (v. 3)

   This is an Eastern saying that means "I will cause you to be ashamed because of the failure of the harvest." Because the harvest would be so bad, the people would become poverty-stricken which caused shame. This shame is that they do not have food to bring to the feasts nor sacrifices to bring to the Temple.

---

[13] IBID. p. 294.

Thoughts

The sins of the men of Judah are at the forefront in this chapter. When one sins that the evil of sins stays with them. It does not matter how large or small the sin is. The bottom line is that sin is sin. Unfortunately, the sin in Judah was self-inflicted. For example, the men the way treating their wives was against God's laws, yet they persisted. Are there laws of God that you regularly break? Then do you request forgiveness from the LORD? The obvious answer from Malachi to the people and to us is stop sinning.

Malachi Chapter Three

Language

New American Standard 1995	Hebrew	Septuagint
1 "Behold, I am going to send My messenger, and he will clear the way before Me. And the Lord, whom you seek, will suddenly come to His temple; and the messenger of the covenant, in whom you delight, behold, He is coming," says	^{WTT} הִנְנִי שֹׁלֵחַ מַלְאָכִי וּפִנָּה־דֶרֶךְ לְפָנָי וּפִתְאֹם יָבוֹא אֶל־הֵיכָלוֹ הָאָדוֹן אֲשֶׁר־אַתֶּם מְבַקְשִׁים וּמַלְאַךְ הַבְּרִית אֲשֶׁר־אַתֶּם חֲפֵצִים הִנֵּה־בָא אָמַר יְהוָה צְבָאוֹת׃ 2 וּמִי מְכַלְכֵּל אֶת־יוֹם בּוֹאוֹ וּמִי	Behold, I send forth my messenger, and he shall survey the way before me: and the Lord, whom ye seek, shall suddenly come into his temple, even the angel of the covenant, whom ye take pleasure in: behold, he is coming, saith the Lord Almighty. 2 And who will abide the day of his coming? or

the LORD of hosts.

2 "But who can endure the day of His coming? And who can stand when He appears? For He is like a refiner's fire and like fullers' soap.

3 "He will sit as a smelter and purifier of silver, and He will purify the sons of Levi and refine them like gold and silver, so that they may present to the LORD offerings in righteousness.

4 "Then the offering of

הָעֹמֵד בְּהֵרָאוֹתוֹ כִּי־הוּא כְּאֵשׁ מְצָרֵף וּכְבֹרִית מְכַבְּסִים: 3 וְיָשַׁב מְצָרֵף וּמְטַהֵר כֶּסֶף וְטִהַר אֶת־בְּנֵי־לֵוִי וְזִקַּק אֹתָם כַּזָּהָב וְכַכֶּסֶף וְהָיוּ לַיהֹוָה מַגִּישֵׁי מִנְחָה בִּצְדָקָה: 4 וְעָרְבָה לַיהֹוָה מִנְחַת יְהוּדָה וִירוּשָׁלָ͏ם כִּימֵי עוֹלָם וּכְשָׁנִים קַדְמֹנִיֹּות: 5 וְקָרַבְתִּי אֲלֵיכֶם

who will withstand at his appearing? for he is coming in as the fire of a furnace and as the herb of fullers.

3 He shall sit to melt and purify as it were silver, and as it were gold: and he shall purify the sons of Levi, and refine them as gold and silver, and they shall offer to the Lord an offering in righteousness.

4 And the sacrifice of Juda and Jerusalem shall be pleasing to

Judah and Jerusalem will be pleasing to the LORD as in the days of old and as in former years. ⁵ "Then I will draw near to you for judgment; and I will be a swift witness against the sorcerers and against the adulterers and against those who swear falsely, and against those who oppress the wage earner in his wages, the widow and the orphan, and those who turn aside the alien and do	לַמִּשְׁפָּט וְהָיִיתִי עֵד מְמַהֵר בַּמְכַשְּׁפִים וּבַמְנָאֲפִים וּבַנִּשְׁבָּעִים לַשָּׁקֶר וּבְעֹשְׁקֵי שְׂכַר־שָׂכִיר אַלְמָנָה וְיָתוֹם וּמַטֵּי־גֵר וְלֹא יְרֵאוּנִי אָמַר יְהוָה צְבָאוֹת: ⁶ כִּי אֲנִי יְהוָה לֹא שָׁנִיתִי וְאַתֶּם בְּנֵי־יַעֲקֹב לֹא כְלִיתֶם: ⁷ לְמִימֵי אֲבֹתֵיכֶם סַרְתֶּם מֵחֻקַּי וְלֹא שְׁמַרְתֶּם שׁוּבוּ אֵלַי וְאָשׁוּבָה	the Lord, according to the former days, and according to the former years. ⁵ And I will draw near to you in judgment; and I will be a sift witness against the witches, and against the adulteresses, and against them that swear falsely by my name, and against them that keep back the hireling's wages, and them that oppress the widow, and afflict

not fear Me," says the LORD of hosts.

6 "For I, the LORD, do not change; therefore you, O sons of Jacob, are not consumed.

7 "From the days of your fathers you have turned aside from My statutes and have not kept *them*. Return to Me, and I will return to you," says the LORD of hosts. "But you say, 'How shall we return?'

8 "Will a man rob God? Yet

אֲלֵיכֶם אָמַר יְהֹוָה צְבָאוֹת וַאֲמַרְתֶּם בַּמֶּה נָשׁוּב: 8 הֲיִקְבַּע אָדָם אֱלֹהִים כִּי אַתֶּם קֹבְעִים אֹתִי וַאֲמַרְתֶּם בַּמֶּה קְבַעֲנוּךָ הַמַּעֲשֵׂר וְהַתְּרוּמָה: 9 בַּמְּאֵרָה אַתֶּם נֵאָרִים וְאֹתִי אַתֶּם קֹבְעִים הַגּוֹי כֻּלּוֹ: 10 הָבִיאוּ אֶת־כָּל־הַמַּעֲשֵׂר אֶל־בֵּית הָאוֹצָר וִיהִי טֶרֶף בְּבֵיתִי

orphans, and that wrest the judgment of the stranger, and fear not me, saith the Lord Almighty.

6 For I am the Lord your God, and I am not changed:

7 but ye, the sons of Jacob, have not refrained from the iniquities of your fathers: ye have perverted my statutes, and have not kept them. Return to me, and I will return to you, saith the Lord Almighty. But ye said,

you are robbing Me! But you say, 'How have we robbed You?' In tithes and offerings.

9 "You are cursed with a curse, for you are robbing Me, the whole nation *of you*!

10 "Bring the whole tithe into the storehouse, so that there may be food in My house, and test Me now in this," says the LORD of hosts, "if I will not open for you the windows of heaven and pour out for

וּבְחָנוּנִי נָא בָּזֹאת אָמַר יְהוָה צְבָאוֹת אִם־לֹא אֶפְתַּח לָכֶם אֵת אֲרֻבּוֹת הַשָּׁמַיִם וַהֲרִיקֹתִי לָכֶם בְּרָכָה עַד־בְּלִי־דָי: 11 וְגָעַרְתִּי לָכֶם בָּאֹכֵל וְלֹא־יַשְׁחִת לָכֶם אֶת־פְּרִי הָאֲדָמָה וְלֹא־תְשַׁכֵּל לָכֶם הַגֶּפֶן בַּשָּׂדֶה אָמַר יְהוָה צְבָאוֹת: 12 וְאִשְּׁרוּ אֶתְכֶם כָּל־הַגּוֹיִם כִּי־תִהְיוּ אַתֶּם אֶרֶץ חֵפֶץ

Wherein shall we return?

8 Will a man insult God? for ye insult me. But ye say, Wherein have we insulted thee? In that the tithes and first-fruits are with you *still*.

9 And ye do surely look off from me, and ye insult me.

10 The year is completed, and ye have brought all the produce into the storehouses; but there shall be the plunder thereof in its house: return now on this behalf, saith

you a blessing until it overflows.

11 "Then I will rebuke the devourer for you, so that it will not destroy the fruits of the ground; nor will your vine in the field cast *its grapes*," says the LORD of hosts.

12 "All the nations will call you blessed, for you shall be a delightful land," says the LORD of hosts.

13 "Your words have been arrogant against Me,"

אָמַר יְהוָה צְבָאוֹת: ס 13 חִזְקוּ עָלַי דִּבְרֵיכֶם אָמַר יְהוָה וַאֲמַרְתֶּם מַה־נִּדְבַּרְנוּ עָלֶיךָ: 14 אֲמַרְתֶּם שָׁוְא עֲבֹד אֱלֹהִים וּמַה־בֶּצַע כִּי שָׁמַרְנוּ מִשְׁמַרְתּוֹ וְכִי הָלַכְנוּ קְדֹרַנִּית מִפְּנֵי יְהוָה צְבָאוֹת: 15 וְעַתָּה אֲנַחְנוּ מְאַשְּׁרִים זֵדִים גַּם־נִבְנוּ עֹשֵׂי רִשְׁעָה גַּם בָּחֲנוּ אֱלֹהִים וַיִּמָּלֵטוּ:

the Lord Almighty, *see* if I will not open to you the torrents of heaven, and pour out my blessing upon you, until ye are satisfied.

11 And I will appoint food for you, and I will not destroy the fruit of your land; and your vine in the field shall not fail, saith the Lord Almighty.

12 And all nations shall call you blessed: for ye shall be a desirable land,

says the LORD. "Yet you say, 'What have we spoken against You?'

14 "You have said, 'It is vain to serve God; and what profit is it that we have kept His charge, and that we have walked in mourning before the LORD of hosts?

15 'So now we call the arrogant blessed; not only are the doers of wickedness built up but they also test

16 אָז נִדְבְּרוּ יִרְאֵי יְהוָה אִישׁ אֶת־רֵעֵהוּ וַיַּקְשֵׁב יְהוָה וַיִּשְׁמָע וַיִּכָּתֵב סֵפֶר זִכָּרוֹן לְפָנָיו לְיִרְאֵי יְהוָה וּלְחֹשְׁבֵי שְׁמוֹ: 17 וְהָיוּ לִי אָמַר יְהוָה צְבָאוֹת לַיּוֹם אֲשֶׁר אֲנִי עֹשֶׂה סְגֻלָּה וְחָמַלְתִּי עֲלֵיהֶם כַּאֲשֶׁר יַחְמֹל אִישׁ עַל־בְּנוֹ הָעֹבֵד אֹתוֹ: 18 וְשַׁבְתֶּם וּרְאִיתֶם בֵּין צַדִּיק

saith the Lord Almighty.

13 Ye have spoken grievous words against me, saith the Lord. Yet ye said, Wherein have we spoken against thee?

14 Ye said, He that serves God labours in vain: and what have we gained in that we have kept his ordinances, and in that we have walked as suppliants before the face of the Lord Almighty?

15 And now we pronounce strangers

God and escape.'"

16 Then those who feared the LORD spoke to one another, and the LORD gave attention and heard *it*, and a book of remembrance was written before Him for those who fear the LORD and who esteem His name.

17 "They will be Mine," says the LORD of hosts, "on the day that I prepare *My* own possession, and I will spare them as a man

לְרָשָׁע בֵּין עֹבֵד אֱלֹהִים לַאֲשֶׁר לֹא עֲבָדוֹ: ס 19 כִּי־הִנֵּה הַיּוֹם בָּא בֹּעֵר כַּתַּנּוּר וְהָיוּ כָל־זֵדִים וְכָל־עֹשֵׂה רִשְׁעָה קַשׁ וְלִהַט אֹתָם הַיּוֹם הַבָּא אָמַר יְהוָה צְבָאוֹת אֲשֶׁר לֹא־יַעֲזֹב לָהֶם שֹׁרֶשׁ וְעָנָף: 20 וְזָרְחָה לָכֶם יִרְאֵי שְׁמִי שֶׁמֶשׁ צְדָקָה וּמַרְפֵּא בִּכְנָפֶיהָ וִיצָאתֶם וּפִשְׁתֶּם

blessed; and all they who act unlawfully are built up; and they have resisted God, and *yet* have been delivered.

16 Thus spoke they that feared the Lord, every one to his neighbour: and the Lord gave heed, and hearkened, and he wrote a book of remembrance before him for them that feared the Lord and reverenced his name.

17 And they shall be mine,

spares his own son who serves him."

¹⁸ So you will again distinguish between the righteous and the wicked, between one who serves God and one who does not serve Him.

כְּעֶגְלֵי מַרְבֵּק׃ ²¹ וְעַסּוֹתֶם רְשָׁעִים כִּי־יִהְיוּ אֵפֶר תַּחַת כַּפּוֹת רַגְלֵיכֶם בַּיּוֹם אֲשֶׁר אֲנִי עֹשֶׂה אָמַר יְהוָה צְבָאוֹת׃ פ ²² זִכְרוּ תּוֹרַת מֹשֶׁה עַבְדִּי אֲשֶׁר צִוִּיתִי אוֹתוֹ בְחֹרֵב עַל־כָּל־יִשְׂרָאֵל חֻקִּים וּמִשְׁפָּטִים׃ ²³ הִנֵּה אָנֹכִי שֹׁלֵחַ לָכֶם אֵת אֵלִיָּה הַנָּבִיא לִפְנֵי בּוֹא יוֹם יְהוָה

saith the Lord Almighty, in the day which I appoint for a peculiar possession; and I will make choice of them, as a man makes choice of his son that serves him.

¹⁸ Then shall ye return, and discern between the righteous and the wicked, and between him that serves God, and him that serves *him* not.

	הַגָּדֹול וְהַנֹּורָא׃ 24 וְהֵשִׁיב לֵב־אָבֹות עַל־בָּנִים וְלֵב בָּנִים עַל־אֲבֹותָם פֶּן־אָבֹוא וְהִכֵּיתִי אֶת־הָאָרֶץ חֵרֶם׃	

Process of Discovery

Linguistics Section

Linguistic Structure

[Action] [1] "Behold, I am going to send My messenger, and he will clear the way before Me. And the Lord, whom you seek, will suddenly come to His temple; and the messenger of the covenant, in whom you delight, behold, He is coming," says the LORD of hosts.

[Result] [2] "But who can endure the day of His coming? And who can stand when He appears? For He is like a refiner's fire and like fullers' soap. [3] "He will sit as a smelter and purifier of silver, and He will purify the sons of Levi and refine them like gold and silver, so that they may present to the LORD offerings in righteousness.

A [4] "Then the offering of Judah and Jerusalem will be pleasing to the LORD as in the days of old and as in former years.

B [5] "Then I will draw near to you for judgment; and I will be a swift witness against the sorcerers and against the adulterers and against those who swear falsely, and against those who oppress the wage earner in his wages, the widow and the orphan, and those who turn aside the alien and do not fear Me," says the LORD of hosts.

C [6] "For I, the LORD, do not change; therefore you, O sons of Jacob, are not consumed. [7] "From the days of your fathers you have turned aside from My statutes and have not kept *them*. Return to Me, and I will return to you," says the LORD of hosts. "But you say, 'How shall we return?' [8] "Will a man rob God? Yet you are robbing Me! But you say, 'How have we robbed You?' In tithes and offerings. [9] "You are cursed with a curse, for you are robbing Me, the whole nation *of you*!

A' [10] "Bring the whole tithe into the storehouse, so that there may be food in My house, and test Me now in this," says the LORD of hosts, "if I will not open for you the windows of heaven and pour out for you a blessing until it overflows.

B' [11] "Then I will rebuke the devourer for you, so that it will not destroy the fruits of the ground; nor will your vine in the field cast *its grapes*," says the LORD of hosts.

C' [12] "All the nations will call you blessed, for you shall be a delightful land," says the LORD of hosts.

[A: offerings, B: judgment vs. blessings, C: return to God]

A [13] "Your words have been arrogant against Me," says the LORD. "Yet you say, 'What have we spoken against You?' [14] "You have said, 'It is vain to serve God; and what profit is it that we have kept His charge, and that we have walked in mourning before the LORD of hosts? [15] 'So now we call the arrogant blessed; not only are the doers of wickedness built up but they also test God and escape.'"

B [16] Then those who feared the LORD spoke to one another, and the LORD gave attention and heard *it*, and a book of remembrance was written before Him for those who fear the LORD and who esteem His name. [17] "They will be Mine," says the LORD of hosts, "on the day that I prepare *My* own possession, and I will spare them as a man spares his own son who serves him."

A [18] So you will again distinguish between the righteous and the wicked, between one who serves God and one who does not serve Him.

[A: righteous and wicked, B: reverence to the LORD]

Discussion

This chapter commences with an action of the LORD and the results, followed by two chiasms. The first part of the chapter speaks about the "Day of the LORD" when the LORD returns to the Earth and judgment of all people alive and dead will begin.

Questioning the Passage

1. Who is the messenger from the LORD? (v. 1)

The people questioned the LORD about the judgment of the wicked in the world. They received the answer. The LORD is going to send a messenger who will usher in the time of judgment. This time will be known as the Final Redemption (Metzudos).[14] Many Christians consider Yeshua to be the messenger spoken of here. However, Yeshua did not usher in a time of judgment. His work brought the Kingdom of God to Earth. Perhaps the Kingdom of God needs to be established on Earth before the LORD will return. The paving of the way for the return of

---

[14] Scherman, Nosson, Meir Zlotowitz, Sheah Brander, and Menachem Davis. "Micah." In The Prophets: The Later Prophets with a Commentary Anthologized from the Rabbinic Writings. Brooklyn, NY: Mesorah Publications, 2013. p. 501.

the LORD could have been started by Yeshua the Messiah. Perhaps Yeshua is the one to pave the way for the LORD.

2. Why will the messenger from the LORD be coming to the Temple? (v. 1)

   The traditional belief is that the messenger from the LORD will come to the Temple in Jerusalem in order to make himself known to the world. If Yeshua is this messenger, Messiah ben Yosef (Ibn Ezra), then Yeshua's entry into Jerusalem and subsequent actions at the Temple are prophesied here. Yeshua brought a message of love, peace, and grace into a violent world. He suffered the same fate as most of God's prophets.

   The messenger of the covenant is the Messianic King (Yeshua) (Radak) or

Elijah, the prophet who was given the title of the Angel of the Covenant for his zealousness in reaffirming the covenant of circumcision (Radak, Metzudos).

The people prayed for the return of Elijah because the prophets foretold the Messiah would follow him and the restoration of the Kingdom of Israel would occur. The onset of the Final Redemption would then occur.

3. What is going to happen when the messenger from the LORD comes? (v. 2) The messenger from the LORD will begin the preparations on Earth for the LORD. It is important that all sinners repent and confess their sins before the LORD's arrival. When we read the Gospels of Yeshua, the return of the

LORD is important to prepare for because judgment is coming.

4. What does the simile "refiner's fire" mean? (v. 2)

The refiner's fire heats metals, like silver, in order to remove the impurities from it. The refiner's fire in us will remove our impurities, which are our sins.

5. What does the simile "fuller's soap" mean? (v. 2)

Another translation for כָּבַס is launderer. This simile has the same meaning as "refiner's fire" so, washed clean

6. What might the reforms to the Priests (descendants of Levi) be? (v. 3)

The messenger of the LORD will remove the corruption of the Priests of Israel.

Perhaps the priests were not insistent to the people about the tithes and offerings that were required by the Torah. If so, they were not correcting the people as the LORD required of them. In order to reform the workings of the Temple system, the leadership of the Temple system needs to be purged first.

7. What is the connection between the LORD never changing and the children of Jacob not perishing? (v. 6)

The LORD is saying that He does not change. Why is the LORD now discussing punishing the children of Jacob? They had been committing sins against the LORD for some time. Radak tells us that the LORD had patience with the sins of Israel hoping His prophets would change the people's ways. Since that process was failing, it was time for the LORD to step in and punish the sinners.[15]

8. How were the people robbing God with their tithes and offerings? (v. 8)

    The tithes of the LORD were considered God's property. Stealing from the LORD is when the people do not give their first tenth to God's representatives, the Priests.

9. What is the curse of verse nine?

    The curse is not defined. The reason for the curse is that of the sins of the people, especially because they are robbing God by not giving back to the LORD the required tithe.

---

[15] IBID. p. 503.

10. Why were the people seeking a profit from keeping the commandments of the LORD? (v. 14)

Even today, people who serve the LORD with their service and tithe from time to time seek a profit. Is it fair that a tither and faithful worshiper of the LORD has less, material wise, than one who violates God's laws? Perhaps the answer lies in the question; What do you expect from God? The people in Malachi's day were questioning why they should give the Priests the required tithing when they were not seeing any results.

11. How were the wicked "built up" and what happened that they "tested God and escaped?"

Materialistically, people who do not follow the Laws of the LORD can create wealth and a good life for themselves. Unfortunately for them, these people do not understand that material gains in life cannot be transferred to the spiritual life in Heaven. Yeshua said it is better to store treasures in heaven than it is to have treasures on earth. If one acquires power and materialism on Earth by breaking the Laws of the LORD, they will discover on judgment day that they may not become a part of the Kingdom of God.

12. What is the symbolism of a man sparing his own son who serves him? (v. 17)

This is from Psalm 103.

> [13] Just as a father has compassion on *his* children, So the LORD has compassion on those who fear Him. (Ps. 103:13 NAU)

This verse tells us that the LORD is like a father who will forgive his children even if they commit a sin against him.

Main/Center Point

This chapter deals with the people not making the proper sacrifices and offerings to the LORD. The tithe from the people biblically is defined as ten percent of income. The Levite priests would collect the tithes and offerings for the work of the LORD and for the sustenance of the priesthood. However, it is clear in this time period that the people of God were not offering the proper tithing. The language is quite strong in verse eight and nine about what would happen when the people robbed the LORD. How? By neglecting to provide the proper tithes, sacrifices, and offerings.

Metaphors

1. What is the book of remembrance? (v. 16) "This is clearly a metaphoric expression used to portray how every single deed is known to God (Abarbanel), for it is obvious that God does not forget and needs no reminder (Radak)."[16]

Scripture cross references

Verse 2   Isa 33:14; Eze 22:14; Rev 6:17; Zec 13:9; Mat 3:10-12; 1Co 3:13-15

Verse 3   Isa 33:14; Eze 22:14; Rev 6:17; Zec 13:9; Mat 3:10-12; 1Co 3:13-15

Verse 4   Psa 51:17-19; 2Ch 7:1-3, 2Ch 7:12

Verse 5   Psa 51:17-19; 2Ch 7:1-3, 2Ch 7:12

Verse 7   Jer 7:25, Jer 7:26; Jer 16:11, Jer 16:12; Zec 1:3

---

[16] IBID. p 507.

Verse 8   Neh 13:11, Neh 13:12

Verse 10 Lev 27:30; Num 18:21-24; Deu 12:6; Deu 14:22-29; Neh 13:12; Psa 78:23-29; Eze 34:26; Lev 26:3-5

Verse 11 Joe 1:4; Joe 2:25

Verse 15 Isa 2:22; Mal 4:1; Jer 7:10

Thoughts

The concentration of this chapter is the evil that was happening because the people were not following the laws and commandments of the LORD that they agreed to at Mount Sinai. The priests are called out because they were the teachers and enforcers of God's commandments. The example used is the tithing that was not being brought into the Temple. The Torah calls for ten percent of income to be given back to the LORD as a tithe. Today, most of the people in Yeshua's churches do not give a tithe, ten percent, to the LORD. Also, the attitude of church goers is that they are giving to their church, not to God. Many people also rate the church and the pastor's sermons to decide what they are "willing to pay for it." This lack of understanding comes from the preachers being told by their church leadership that tithing and money are not to be spoken as a sermon. Sadly, this is happening in many churches. One day those who cheat the LORD's tithe will discover what lies ahead.

Malachi Chapter Four

Language

New American Standard 1995		Septuagint
[1] For behold, the day is coming, burning like a furnace; and all the arrogant and every evildoer will be chaff; and the day that is coming will set them ablaze," says the LORD of hosts, "so that it will leave them neither root nor branch." [2] "But for you who fear My name, the sun of righteousness will rise with		For, behold, a day comes burning as an oven, and it shall consume them; and all the aliens, and all that do wickedly, shall be stubble: and the day that is coming shall set them on fire, saith the Lord Almighty, and there shall not be left of them root or branch. [2] But to you that fear my name shall the Sun of righteousness arise, and healing *shall be* in his

healing in its wings; and you will go forth and skip about like calves from the stall.

3 "You will tread down the wicked, for they will be ashes under the soles of your feet on the day which I am preparing," says the LORD of hosts.

4 "Remember the law of Moses My servant, *even the* statutes and ordinances which I commanded him in Horeb for all Israel.

5 "Behold, I am going to send you Elijah the

wings: and ye shall go forth, and bound as young calves let loose from bonds.

3 And ye shall trample the wicked; for they shall be ashes underneath your feet in the day which I appoint, saith the Lord Almighty.

4

5 And, behold, I will send to you Elias the Thesbite, before the great and glorious day of the Lord comes;

6 who shall turn again the heart of the father to the son, and the heart of a man to his neighbour, lest I come and smite

prophet before the coming of the great and terrible day of the LORD. ⁶ "He will restore the hearts of the fathers to *their* children and the hearts of the children to their fathers, so that I will not come and smite the land with a curse."		the earth grievously. Remember the law of my servant Moses, accordingly as I charged him *with it* in Choreb for all Israel, *even* the commandments and ordinances.

SPECIAL NOTE: Malachi 4:1-6 are a part of chapter three in the Hebrew version.

Process of Discovery

Linguistics Section

Linguistic Structure

[Evildoers] [1] For behold, the day is coming, burning like a furnace; and all the arrogant and every evildoer will be chaff; and the day that is coming will set them ablaze," says the LORD of hosts, "so that it will leave them neither root nor branch."

[The Messiah] [2] "But for you who fear My name, the sun of righteousness will rise with healing in its wings; and you will go forth and skip about like calves from the stall. [3] "You will tread down the wicked, for they will be ashes under the soles of your feet on the day which I am preparing," says the LORD of hosts. [4] "Remember the law of Moses My servant, *even the* statutes and ordinances which I commanded him in Horeb for all Israel. [5] "Behold, I am going to send you Elijah the prophet before the coming of the great and terrible day of the LORD. [6] "He will restore the hearts of the fathers to *their* children and the hearts of the children to their fathers, so that I will not come and smite the land with a curse."

Discussion

This chapter comprises two statements. The first statement is about what was going to happen to the evil people of the land. The second statement is about the coming of the Messiah, who was going to restore justice to the righteous.

People's names

1. אֵלִיָּה *Eliyyah* **Meaning:** 'Yah is God,' a well-known prophet of Israel, also three other Israelites.

Name of places

1. חֹרֵב *Choreb* **Meaning:** 'waste,' a mountain in Sinai

Culture Section

Discussion

Wood is scarce in the Middle East and coal was unknown. Therefore, people would gather stubbles and chaff to be used to heat their ovens. The wicked are likened to the chaff, which is consumed daily by the oven.

"Healing in its wings" means that justice and righteousness were going to reign in the land. The LORD was going to heal the brokenhearted and bring illumination to the gloom of Israel's affliction.[17]

---

[17] Errico, Rocco A., and George M. Lamsa. "Malachi Chapter One." In Aramaic Light on Ezekiel, Daniel, and the Minor Prophets: A Commentary Based on the Aramaic Language and Ancient Near Eastern Customs. Smyma, GA: Noohra Foundation, 2012.

Thoughts

The final parts of chapters three and four point to the coming of the Messiah. That is why the church bishops, who determined the order of the books of the Bible, placed Malachi directly before Matthew.

Bibliography

Errico Rocco, George Lamsa. 2012. *Aramaic Light on Ezekiel, Daniel, and the Minor Prophets*. Smyma, GA: Noohra Foundation.

Jones, Howell. n.d. *Remembering a Forgotten Covenant*. Accessed March 28, 2017. http://www.wscal.edu/resource-center/remembering-a-forgotten-covenant.

n.d. *Malachi Chiasms*. Accessed March 18, 2017. http://www.bible.literarystructure.info/bible/39_Malachi_pericope_e.html#1 .

Scherman, Noson, and Meir Zlotowitz. 203. *Isaiah: The later prophets with a commentary*. Brooklyn, NY: Mesorah Publications.